The York Journal.
Issue #1

Copyright © The York Journal, 2021. All rights reserved.
No reproduction, copy or transmission, in whole or in part, may be made without written permission.
Cover Image: 'Island' - © artepicturas

The York Journal, Issue #1.
Editor & Publisher: Luke Downing.
Illustrations: Holly Barratt, Marina Phoont, Mim Robson.
Design consultant: Emily Greenman.

ISBN 978-1-5272-9318-2

www.theyorkjournal.com

All enquiries to: editor@theyorkjournal.com

Contents

♦

5	**Introduction**
9	**Hekla** | Amy Stewart
19	**Queen Wasp** | Emily Black
24	**The Fox** | Daniel Gustafsson
27	**Burst** | Lauren Sharp
30	**Seen** | Rosie Driffill
37	**24 Hours in a Ghost Town** | Alicia V McClane
51	**Collection** | Neil James Hudson
56	**Galaxies** | Laura Turner
59	**Leaving May** | Robert Powell
73	**Beyond the Storm** | Kitty Greenbrown
77	**The Artist** | Amy Farrar

Introduction

◆

Thank you, reader, for opening the pages of this very first issue of *The York Journal*. Since our call for submissions back in November, I've had the privilege of reading hundreds of entries from new writers exploring their developing craft, and established writers excited to support a new publication.

As is the cliché of our time, *The York Journal* was born of too many lockdown hours indoors, as the world of the written word replaced the one being shuttered away. Subscriptions to various quarterly literary reviews and journals mounted, but none from my hometown.

During this period, I had the pleasure of interviewing (via Zoom, naturally) many of York's creative thinkers and enablers for a film project exploring our city's culture strategy. While speaking to Mat Lazenby, the creative force behind *LazenbyBrown* and a key figure in York's creative scene, something he said stood out to me:

"York can be the city you want it to be. The things that you want might not be there, so you have to make them."

And so, I did. With the help of some creative friends, the call for submissions went out, the first writers were selected, and these pages were printed.

Through this publication, we hope to shine a light on the incredible literary voices in this city by regularly publishing their work alongside global writers and, in time, building a readership of people hungry for new writing. Creativity is the perfect response to a year of change and unquestionable hardship, and many others in the city seem to be responding in the same way. Theatres are bouncing back with work from local creatives, and we've even had other journals launch and relaunch*, proving that the creative heart of our community is beating hard.

Issue #1 of *The York Journal* opens with Amy Stewart's short story, *Hekla*, where we find a woman setting out on a climb across an unforgiving landscape as she journeys towards healing and acceptance.

With that, I'd like to thank you one more time for your support, and leave the rest over to our talented writers.

Luke Downing | Editor

---

*See also: York St John University's annual publication, *York Literary Review*, amongst others.

"Hekla hulks before me,
domed and snow-topped…"

Hekla

Amy Stewart

◆

'Why have you come here?' the man asks, emphasis on the "you". His English is impeccable; the words made playful and new by his accent. Still, there's no mistaking I'm being admonished. 'You tourists – you have no idea how dangerous the volcano actually is.'

'I have to see it.'

'Can't you just take a picture? From a distance?'

I shake my head. 'I'm climbing it because my friend did. Last year.'

He seems to understand, then. He breathes in deeply, hands me my bottle of water and says, 'That'll be 400 króna.'

I pay and leave the shop before he can see the chunk that those simple words have taken out of me. I need to get better at talking about it – about you.

After months of preparation, here I finally am, at the Hekla trailhead. It used to be one of the most hiked trails in Iceland, but it's quiet today, despite the shopkeeper's complaints of tourists. The hike will take me two days, so I've packed to camp. I couldn't get the tent poles to fold properly so one juts accusingly, damningly, out of the side of my pack. You'd grin at that.

I often summon the nuances that animated you, recite them like a litany – the kink in your curls, the freckle on your Adam's apple, the way your eyes were always puffy when you woke up – but they feel flat as photographs. People have told me to stop pulling at the same fraying seam. To find a proper way to say goodbye to you.

Hekla hulks before me, domed and snow-topped, sloping sides coated with gravel and scree. I pause at the first signpost and drink some water. I wish for a ceremonial catalyst– an albatross overhead, or someone to slap my back, urge me on – but there's just me. Me and the path that'll take me upward, all the way up to the place where you died.

◆

It's been a long time since I've hiked anywhere. My lungs remind me of that after about an hour and a half, aching as though they're filled with water. There's a lick of sweat under my headband, despite the fact that it's March and most likely below freezing. I look back the way I've come and am disheartened that I can still see the trailhead. Someone else is down there, starting their hike. My watch says it's 12:05pm. I press on.

I was at a friend's barbecue when your mum phoned me. I took the call in the cool of the house and walked back out feeling blistered. I didn't tell anyone – no one there knew you. Instead, I drank a gin and tonic and talked about Wimbledon, and then when it was acceptable, I went home. I lay on top of the sheets, fully dressed and not quite crying, until your mum called again and said she needed help planning the funeral.

The path breaks its bones into switchbacks which lead gradually up a steep pass. I put my head down, shins burning. How did you feel when you walked here? Did you relish the cold air in your lungs? Your laugh returns to me, unbidden. Your whole body shook when you laughed. You'd always spill a bit of your drink, wine sloshing out of the glass.

I spot a bench formed out of worn stone and decide to take my first break. I chew on a protein bar, tasting nothing, aware of a ragged noise alongside the wind. A man crests the hill and salutes as he approaches. He must be around my age – maybe a little younger – and has the stringy arms and legs of someone who has run or exercised hard all their life. He looks like the kind of person who talks about energy gel at dinner parties.

'Good afternoon,' he calls. I nod and look away, but it doesn't deter him. 'You must be mad too, then? To take on Hekla?' He half-laughs it, casting an eye over my small pack, the way my chest is – still – heaving up and down. He has the flattish vowels of the Midlands. They sound forced out here. 'You're a keen walker?'

'Not at all,' I say.

He frowns. 'It's a fairly steep hike. I'm guessing you know about the last eruption at least?'

That word. I tuck damp hair behind my ear. 'Yes, I know about that,' is all I can bring myself to say.

'Ten people,' he says, shaking his head. 'Awful.'

Unrecognisable. Bones like melted plastic.

'Eleven,' I reply.

It strikes me, maybe for the first time, that this is where it actually happened. This ground. Parts of you might still be in the air. In the dirt. My fingers tighten on the stone beneath my legs. My temple throbs, and I realise I've gritted my teeth into a gate.

'Want a little company?' the man asks, and I wonder what it is about my crossed legs and reticence that suggests that.

'No, thank you. I think I'd rather walk by myself.' The words come out surprisingly easily. It's making me bold, being here. Knowing you're close.

The man holds both palms up by his waist and shrugs, almost as if to say, your loss. He makes a motion that looks like doffing his cap. 'Good luck,' he says, not unkindly, then walks on. His whistle carries on the wind. I wait for ten minutes or so until he's safely ahead of me – though there's little chance of me catching up – before I, too, set off.

I remember when you first told me you were coming to Iceland. A once-in-a-career opportunity to study one of the country's most active stratovolcanoes – I remember that, word for word. There was no stopping you. There never was; it was a quality I saw the first day I met you, in the grubby foyer of our halls at Liverpool Uni. You told me that morning, with all the conviction of someone holy, that we would be friends until the day one of us died. You were right.

I've hit a rhythm of kinds now. My breathing has deepened, as if my lungs are hiding a secret shelf that I could never reach before. My arms swing side to side, helping to balance me as I navigate rocks – half-submerged in the ground like icebergs – and thick, packed mud. I've been walking for four hours when I hit the first patch of snow. The sharpness of the sun makes it sparkle, like stardust sprinkled on the rough earth. Peaking a hand over my eyes, I look up, see how the path becomes snowier and snowier on the ascent. Of course, I'd seen Hekla's white peak from pictures, from the trailhead – but it only strikes me as odd now that a volcano should be topped by ice. I think of the lava tubes beneath my feet, the thick veins of fire, spluttering with flesh-melting power.

After another couple of hours, the sky blanches pink, and I know I need to start thinking about setting up camp. I did read up on how to do it – it needs to be somewhere flat, sheltered, ideally near water – but standing here surrounded by snow and gravel, I feel clueless and woefully unprepared. The air has gained a bite that gnaws at my toes, my cheeks, and I suddenly wonder whether there are animals out here, this high up. The notion of sleeping out in the open, with all that fire underneath, seems ridiculous. I can't quite summon the motivation to unpack my bag. My fingers flex, useless with cold.

What would you say, if you could see me now? You'd laugh. You'd say, it's just a fucking tent. Rough language always suited your tongue, somehow.

I shake my shoulders a bit to get the blood pumping and settle on a little patch off the path beneath the skeleton of a tree. It's better than nothing. It takes me half an hour to assemble the tent, and even then, the hooks won't stay in the ground – the dirt is too fine, too flimsy. The tent shifts with every breath of wind. It's almost completely dark by the time it even occurs to me that I should have started a fire. I sit in the mouth of the tent, palms braced against my forehead.

You were so happy here. I used to look forward to the pictures you sent; the desolate, sweeping landscapes of moss and stone. Once, even the northern lights: the greens and pinks streaking the sky like the swirls of a paintbrush. You'd tell me what the rocks had revealed to you through their marks and texture: their old, silent stories.

It is so complete, this dark. Darkness like this just doesn't exist in the city – perhaps nowhere in England. It is pure and resolute as silence, thicker than water. It makes the space around me feel limitless, crushingly so. I long for another human being. I remind myself that you were here, that you live here now, that you are the rocks and the grass and the snow and even the sky – but it's no comfort in this kind of dark.

There's only one light that I can see, behind me, further up the slope. A light that flickers and dances. I pick up my pack and abandon my tent to walk up the hill. I remember the head torch in my bag and manage to don it clumsily. It creates a pale moon-streak on shifting stones.

The man from earlier spots me and waves. He looks friendly but slightly stupid, standing there in the light of the fire, arms above his head.

'Do you come in peace?' he asks with a grin.

I make myself smile and nod. It's worth it to be in his camp. He's built a fire, a proper fire, and something is cooking in foil. His tent is at least twice the size of mine and secured on a solid, flat piece of ground. He's even stretched a tarpaulin between two tree trunks to create a canopy. A tartan blanket is laid out beneath it. He cracks open another beer and hands it to me, mimes "cheers" and takes a thick glug. Without saying anything, he retreats back onto the blanket, propped up on his elbows.

'Is it your first time climbing Hekla?' My voice sounds stronger than it feels, and I'm glad for it.

'Uh-huh. I've done Hvannadalshnúkur, and Esjan. They're both higher, and harder, than Hekla, but… I don't know. There's just something about,' he puts his arm out, still holding his beer, and strokes the shadow of the horizon, 'this. The quiet. Maybe it's knowing about what happened here.' He sniffs and readjusts his position. 'Of course, that's why my friends told me not to come. That there could be another eruption sometime soon, that the last came out of nowhere. I'm sure you were told the same.'

I nod, the beer can cold against my teeth.

'I suppose it just makes me feel more alive. The threat of imminent danger. The thought that we could die here. It makes it all more beautiful.'

'Is that supposed to impress me?'

He chuckles, warmly. 'I think so.'

My fingers tighten around my can. I become aware of him moving, and at first, I think he's going to touch me, but he gets up and walks to the fire. With bare hands, he retrieves the foil parcel from the middle and tosses it from one palm to another, lips letting out rapid puffs of air before dropping it into the space between us. He unwraps the foil to reveal a sweet potato, rope-coloured skin neatly charred. As he runs his fork down the middle, fluffy flesh blooms out. Something about it makes me blush. He offers me the fork first, and we take it in turns, eating in a silence that isn't uncomfortable. Once we've finished, the man yawns and cracks his neck.

'I better turn in. Planning an early start to make the summit.'

I nod. I don't know what I'm about to say until the words leave my mouth. 'Can I stay in your tent tonight?'

He stiffens and raises his eyebrows in a way that seems involuntary, his mouth shaping a word and abandoning it. It makes me like him. I don't know what I want him to say. I just can't face walking back down the hill in the dark to my sorry tent with the ghost of you everywhere and nowhere.

'Sure, I mean, if you want to. I'm sorry, I only have one sleeping bag.' Each word he says sounds like a question.

'That's ok,' I reply.

Together we smother the fire. He disappears behind a tree to brush his teeth and relieve himself while I slither down into the sleeping bag in the orange-tinged world of the tent. It smells like the man in here: earthy, spicy, slightly sweaty. When he comes in, he doesn't look at me. As he lowers himself into the sleeping bag – precise about it, careful not to bump my thigh with his – I take the chance to look at him. He's not unattractive, really. His haircut is a bit dated, too long on the sides and at the back, but he's in good shape, and his eyes are clear and sparkling. I place a hand on his stomach, and that seems to be the only invitation he needs.

◆

Later, I wake from a skittish sleep. The hurricane lamp is still on. The man is asleep on his stomach next to me, mouth open against the pillow, blowing sleep-breath in my direction. I creep as carefully as I can to the tent entrance, unzip it, and step out into the dark.

The sky has exploded with stars. My legs are weak and so I stagger beneath them, flattened by their light. And then there's the moon: a slice away from full, an eye in the blackness.

You would have seen this, too. You were halfway up Hekla when it happened, in the middle of the night. It was all so quick, according to the news reports. There was no time to save you or any of your team. You would have stood here, or somewhere close. You would have had thoughts so much more unique and fragile and profound than I'm having now. You would have found a way to craft them, like bending metal, into aching sentences and prose. You were always raw to the beauty of the world. You let it in.

I lie on the ground in front of the tent. It is freezing, and my body has started to tremble, but I don't want to move. There's nothing above me but the sky, the heavy moon climbing, the quiet.

And I feel you, finally, in the night. I'm surrounded by the emptiness that you are now. There's nothing to cling to anymore, but you're as real as the rising moon-tide, timeless and frightening and beautiful all at once.

◆

When I finally open my eyes, it's to a shy dawn. My joints are stiff and painful. I see my tent a little way down the hill, the route which felt so treacherous in the dark seeming innocuous now. As I stand and brush myself off, the tent opens behind me and the man appears, yawning.

'Leaving so soon?' he asks, a questioning tone under the joviality.

'I am,' I reply. 'I'm going to go home now, I think.'

'This isn't the summit, it's another few hours' away.'

'I know.'

He scratches the back of his head and studies me. He doesn't seem to find any answers in my face. 'You've come all the way here, and you're not even going to finish the hike?'

I can see how, to him, this would seem incomprehensible. But there's no point going any further. I don't want to go any higher than you did – I know that, now. I've already found you.

'Good luck with it,' I say, and I mean it. I feel his eyes on me as I walk away.

I watch my hands pack up my tent, feeling as though they're someone else's. I suddenly remember the scar on your left hand, the one in the shape of a "c", a silvery crescent on the hard part between thumb and forefinger. You got it from putting your hands in the middle of two fighting dogs as a little boy. I haven't thought about it in years. I revel in the memory, in its insignificance, and feel grateful.

As I make my way back down Hekla, and the snow gives way to grit, I wonder whether I've said goodbye to you. It felt more like a hello.◆

"I saw the wasp in my dreams for weeks afterwards, dreams of lemon-yellow bodies and infinite legs rubbing abdomens."

Queen Wasp

Emily Black

♦

'Why did you have to kill her?' I said, 'Why couldn't you have put her out the window, or walked her to the end of the garden?'

'It would come back. It was a queen looking for somewhere to hibernate, and I don't want them nesting in the walls or in the roof this summer.'

'You didn't have to kill her.'

'Her,' you chuckled, 'you talk like it's human.'

I pulled a face, unwilling to admit I felt a strange connection to the female wasp that now lay in two halves, black and yellow beads, on the bedside table. The murder weapon: an upturned whisky glass. The lamp was on, and your face half-lit as though in a black-and-white Hitchcock. Your stubble multiplied under the shadows, and your nostrils flared in two slits.

'C'mon sweet pea, let's go to sleep,' you said, pushing your bare chest against me and sticking your hands down your boxers for a scratch. I rolled onto my back, lying above the duvet. You called me that, sweet pea, because I used to buy the flowers to sit on top of the piano, before money got tight.

'Can you please move the wasp first?' I was closest to the bedside table, 'I don't want to sleep with it next to my face.'

You chuckled again. 'It's dead, it can't hurt you.'

'I'm not worried about it hurting me. I just don't want it there.'

'Fine.' You got up reluctantly, pulled back the duvet and moved to the table. I looked away and heard the scrape of the whisky glass as you gathered up the two halves of the female insect. You nodded at the window, and I moved obediently to open it for you. The winter air rushed through the gap, and I pulled my silk dressing gown around my shoulders. I watched as you tossed out the tiny pieces of what had, a matter of minutes ago, been able to reduce a man to tears.

I saw the wasp in my dreams for weeks afterwards, dreams of lemon-yellow bodies and infinite legs rubbing abdomens. Dreams that were textured with confusion, because I didn't know what I wanted, but you served a plate of them for dinner, resting dead in a cool jumble of yellow, wire legs to the sky, with that strange fuzz backlit against the light. We were nowhere, but we sat at a white table, like the one in the restaurant where you asked me to marry you, when I had no one else, and thought yes, I'll take the plate of wasps, so I nodded, and we were engaged.

'She was looking for somewhere to hibernate.'

You shut the window and walked behind me, back to the bed.

'Motherfu—' You gripped me on the shoulder hard, and I buckled to your weight.

'What?' I swivelled around.

'That bloody piano.' You were clutching your big toe—the one with the bunion. 'I keep telling you we should get rid of it. Ow.'

You continued to grip me, and I bent to stroke the toe. It was red and throbbing.

'I kicked the pedal again. Give me a pound for every time I've done that and maybe we wouldn't need to think about selling the damned thing.'

'We're not selling it,' I said under my breath.

Fingers that were once employed in quick motions across the keys, moving up and down the scales and across the spectrum of sound, were now put to use flicking through my pages of subsections, clauses, and case studies. Despite my years of experience, Covid-19 had wiped out my career as a pianist. Concert halls stayed closed, and the arts had sunk like a ship to the bottom of the ocean. It was embarrassing to start again at age thirty-two. I knew you looked down on me for not doing something sensible to begin with, like you did.

'Even if you don't end up doing law, it's a good degree to have,' you'd said, when my application for the conversion course came back successful. 'You can go anywhere with that… get a lot of money.'

I sat, silent, on the piano stool, staring at the open laptop on the closed lid. It was a sacrifice made so that we could have the nice house, maybe a nice wedding once this was over, a good life, but for me, it was so I could keep the piano.

'We should sell it,' you repeated, not hearing my murmuring at your pulsating toe. 'My parents can't bail us out again.'

'I know, I know,' I said, 'but I start the law course in January, then it's a year of training, and I can start earning after that. Just a little longer to hold on.' I stood straight again, giving the toe one last tap.

'Two years.'

'Not long,' I pleaded.

'You don't even practice the bloody thing anymore.'

'I don't have the time,' I said, flashing my canines in a half-smile.

In the dreams that followed, I shook their grey nests, and they were empty. You cleared them out, eating them one by one with a metal fork, plucking antennae from your teeth, dragging them from your gums with wooden picks, metallic shells glinting on your tongue, crushed like Smarties; these wasps whose colonies had the potential to outlive our lineage, or maybe already had, but you opened your mouth and licked your tongue across the white surface of your teeth, and my jaw clenched with fear when yours loosened, opening wider and wider, ready to eat me next.

We got back into bed, and I pressed your toe to see if it hurt. 'Ow,' you moaned, 'it might be broken.'

I wanted to tell you it definitely wasn't broken, but I bit my tongue.

I undid my dressing gown and threw it at the piano stool. It missed and slid off the velvet top, slipping into a pink puddle on the floor.

I turned back to face you, and saw your eyes shift, like a dog who'd spotted a squirrel, from your toe to my camisole pyjama top. I pulled the duvet around me as goosebumps rose on my arms.

You tucked yourself under the covers, and offered to warm me up.

'We should go to sleep,' I said, 'you have work tomorrow. I need to study.'

You kissed me, your stubble like gravel on my chin. I felt so small as I nuzzled your nose with mine. Your hand slid up my bare thigh, to the seam of my pyjama shorts, where it kept going. Your nails skimmed my hip, and carried down to the elastic of my pants, where you stopped, and tugged. Your face was so close to mine that it was as though you had eight eyes.

'How're you feeling sweet-pea?' you said.

'Tired.'

Your hand withdrew from my pants, and you leant back. I lay back on the pillow. You looked as though you'd been stung and, for a moment, I liked it.

'Okay. That's fine. We'll go to sleep.' You pulled the duvet higher, and lay down to face me.

The piano stood neglected in the corner. I saw the reflection of two figures on the bed in the shine of the lacquered top.

Sometimes it was different, and the hives weren't empty, but the papier-mâché bulbs that hung in trees came alive, and I imagined how they would burst from those abandoned homes, the places left because of fumigation, where the large gas tents couldn't reach, and hands with metal forks couldn't pluck them from their sleep. There were nights where I saw them alive, those glass wings that fluttered in swathes between the sweet peas, humming through the sky and parting the air above your white table, the one from the restaurant, and for a moment, that dinner where we'd bound ourselves together, was disturbed, by these hundreds of fragments that formed a delicious cloud in the nothing. They were safe in numbers, and safe behind their sting; something delivered like a pin-prick, executed like the telling of a secret.

In the background, somewhere far away, three notes played on a piano: one, two three, over and over, soft, gentle alongside the humming, over and over. One, two, three.

We lay face to face for a moment, my eyes dusted with sleep, yours, wide and searching. I didn't want to admit I felt an affinity with the queen wasp. She was the only wasp in the hive who'd outlive her entire colony. That must be lonely, I thought. You leant over and turned off the lamp, wrapped your arm around my waist, and squeezed me tight.◆

The Fox

Daniel Gustafsson

◆

He comes, as beauty does,
unbidden, bright against the rain-soaked red
of aged brick. A loping tread
has brought him here, displaced
from provinces' depleted stores
to prowl this urban waste.

A brazen, bushy thing,
a dew-bedraggled coat of harvest moon,
he braves the night; and so, by soon-
dismantled, rusting tracks
of discontinued lines, down one-
way streets and cul-de-sacs,

he comes. Now, unaware
of being seen from half un-blinded spots,
he steals across the parking lots
to ripe, abundant bins –
to root and rummage, ripping shreds,
his muzzle mining tins.

Although, from such a feast
of scraps, this vagrant flame goes hungry still,
he comes, as robins later will
when downfall hides the stars,
to nourish here, unknowingly,
a deeper need of ours.◆

"My reflection smiles in the dark…
Light drapes her in the moment she opens
the door, before she disappears."

Burst

Lauren Sharp

◆

The tomato bursts in my mouth. It tastes sweet and natural. It tastes of goodness. The tree in front of my window swings, skeletal branches rocking. Beyond the crunchy lichen, dry leaves on the road are whipped in circles. I turn from the window and watch my silhouette, a gobo on the opposite wall, it slides off to the left in the shadow of the door frame. I consider another tomato, but I want to save them. A few paces take me from one room to another, down the hallway in the narrow flat. It's dark with the other doors closed, except at night, where blue shines in from the kitchen as you walk back down the hall and you look too long at your pale reflection in the mirror at the other end.

I make that mistake tonight as I go back to my room with water in my favourite glass. I stole it the night you kissed me for the first time. It's patterned with lines crosshatching to create diamonds, a ribbed texture in my hand. The mirror is large for such a narrow wall. It has a silver frame that holds onto the colour of the reflection, so you can't always tell where it ends. Tonight, I have too much time, so I walk past my room and closer to the mirror. How sad I look when my hair gets this length, and that I look like a child in the too-big white shirt and nothing else. I barely have breasts and my eyes are too dark. In the mirror, I look at myself and I am pathetic, until I look too long and I am not. My reflection smiles in the dark. Her hair lies properly, and the white shirt hangs off more of a shape, not the usual unflattering square. Her eyes are big. Her lips are full. She turns away from me, glass in hand and walks a little way down to her room. Light drapes her in the moment she opens the door, before she disappears.

I look again the next day, after a night of worrying I'm too warm and waking up naked but with no one there. The only voice I hear is my voice, the only hands that have touched me are my own. I throw something on, and leave the bed. It's mid-afternoon. I allow myself another tomato. It tastes of the earth, of growing, of outside. On my way back I look in the mirror. My reflection is dressed. She's wearing my clothes, but put together better than I ever could. She has her key in one hand. She turns her face side to side to check her make up, her eyes staring into mine, then turns away again, and pauses at the shoe rack to slide on sandals. I guess it must be summer now. I never noticed my profile before. It's ugly on me. She undoes the chain on the door and slips outside, making sure to put the key back into the lock and pull it shut so it doesn't slam. The frame is empty now, I can see straight down the corridor. I turn into my own room and tell myself I'll be reading.

There are small, good things. Later, I cut the plum tomatoes carefully in half, they hold their shape, still firm. The rich smell clings to my fingertips. I put them in a bowl and take them to my table. I'm grateful for the feel of my feet in the carpet, to straighten my back and for the deep breaths I take. I have so much time to notice the taste of everything.

Now I try not to stop and look too much, or at least look down so that my fringe covers my eyes when I'm walking towards the mirror. But it's hard when that's the only route in a small flat, and I'm dragged again and again back to my own face. It's either look in or look out. Out is too loud, and more so now. All of the people are on the other side of the glass.◆

Seen

Rosie Driffill

◆

It was me

Who introduced the blindman to Versace.

I must have told him about

My Cartier sunglasses, too, because why else

Would he have mentioned them?

Why else would he have asked,

As we drank coffee from blue willow cups,

so you wear them because they are cool

to the touch? Because the rims meet perfectly here

(he touched my nose) and catch the glare

more – shall we say – deftly, than any other pair?

and that dress, which you call red,

because the silk is gentle, inapparent as skin,

with lace about the neck that you can fondle,

protectively, when being seen

feels suddenly – shall we say – difficult?

this is why you wear these, above all others, no?

The Burleigh cups were my grandmother's.

I had begged to have them, to be seen to own them.

The edges were rounded as sea glass, in parts,

And his rising inflection was an accusation,

Not a question; like a foreigner feigning confusion.

He knew exactly why I wore them, and when.

He knew I didn't use the silverware

When I cut a lonely figure, under blueish light

In the kitchen, eating standing up, half listening to Mahler,

Or birdsong, or the news. He knew I wouldn't wear Prada

If I walked out of people's way on the beach.

I knew the colour of the ocean. I had seen

Waves wrap themselves round basalt columns,

Beg their stature from them over time until

Only stumps remained, and I shared that, and I told him

I had also known eyes on me, many eyes at once

And how they had gone up and down, up and down

Until I learned to control what they saw.

He said, so being seen has been painful?

Being seen has been painful, I said,

And these days, when you are seldom seen,

You might put what you want to be seen in a photograph.

He asked me if I remembered

Our trip to the Philharmonie, years ago,

When I took pictures of the sail-like rooves

And the people in the rounds, and he sat for hours

Listening to what I barely remembered as Liszt.

He said, I am curious about what I can't see:

the cellist, the blackbird, blue willow, ocean.

I sometimes bargain for just the one eye. But if seeing meant

learning the shame you might feel when you're seen, or

remembering to be seen to enjoy other senses, believe me,

I'd settle for silverware, a stake, a porcelain shard

to gouge the one eye out, catch it in your grandmother's cup

bleed red as Versace, from here to the shore.

let me know your third eye, he said.

let us seek the third eye, the one that burns beacon bright

beneath our skulls. Let us shed our skins that we might be truly known

cast our photographs into the wind

lay surfaces bare take back the power we wrongly meted out

to those who may use sight to pour scorn.

Oh, to tolerate less than this, to be blind to less than this!

to keep provenance of purchase a secret, perhaps

whisper it into the waves! Won't you join me

in my darkness, to see what I can see?

It was me

Who asked the blindman

If I could take his picture, and I wiped away the coffee rings with my sleeve.

How else would anyone know he'd been here?◆

"...Sullivan hastened to keep up with the light. His heart pounded with the prospects of childish dares."

24 Hours in a Ghost Town

Alicia V McClane

◆

The desert wind lifted sand from the dirt road and whipped it through the car's air conditioning valves. Mr Sullivan slapped the vents closed and brushed sand from his slacks. His eyes felt gritty, and he rubbed them, a habit worsening in the latter end of his 14-hour drive. The sun was creeping up behind the fiery Carnelian mountains, a welcomed sight after navigating dark, unmarked roads through the night. Ahead he saw the town of West Galmore; distant and vacant, it was finally his.

He hadn't expected Mr Wilcox to be waiting for him at this hour, but there he was, sat in his truck by the gates. Mr Sullivan squinted against the sun, unsure whether his eyes deceived him as Mr Wilcox hopped down from his Cruiser with a shotgun tucked under his arm.

'What the hell?' Sullivan breathed the first words from his mouth in a long time, dry and thin like the desert air.

Wilcox made no move to aim the gun. He merely shaded his eyes with his free hand and watched as the car approached. Sullivan had taken his foot off the gas instinctively, but pressed on once the shock subsided. As soon as he was in shouting distance, he lowered the window and waved in what he hoped was a friendly yet assertive way. Wilcox returned a curt back and forth of his left hand, his right still cupping the neck of the shotgun.

'I'm Ray Sullivan. We spoke on the phone.' Sullivan shouted, his voice lacking the confident energy he had hoped for.

Wilcox indicated for him to approach the entrance and set about moving the heavy, wooden gate to the side. The car bumped over the pitted road, Sullivan cursing the city suspension, towards the old man holding the gate. Up close, he didn't look so threatening; his skin baked red-brown from years of labour in the sun, his short, white hair surprisingly neat.

'We get visitors.' Wilcox shouted, nodding at the gun.

Sullivan added a mental note to discuss this further, at a safer time. Wilcox needed to ice his trigger finger before the park opened. Town! He meant town. One of the legal caveats of the purchase had been an agreement to preserve the town's original features, not just to create a tourist hotspot capitalising on the gory history. His stake was definitely in the latter, but there was work to be done before it'd be a viable cash cow.

'Take this road all the way down and I'll meet you at the square.' Wilcox said, tugging his truck open; his voice sounded murky with disuse. They'd also have to work on his people skills if he was going to stay.

There was only one road into town. It couldn't officially be classed as a road on any USA maps, but on this vacant land, a path formed by decades of horse-drawn traffic provided the best route in and out. Sullivan tried to make mental notes about the extensive work that needed to be done to the entrance, but managing the bounce of his car over the potholes was demanding his full attention. He passed a string of wooden shacks, gently leaning towards the mountains, and piles of rusted metal and junk littering the sand. Not quite the entrance he remembered from his visit, but nothing his crew couldn't tidy up. Sullivan stopped the car in front of the large Town Hall, a squat, two-story structure clad with solid timber. It had stood out on the online listing, the moody building reminding Sullivan of the Westerns he'd loved as a child. A fragment of a past world that was going to make him good money after a little sprucing up.

What he had not been prepared for, was the overwhelming smell of rot as soon as he opened the car door. The heat of the day was already creeping in, and unfamiliar smells of the desert hung thickly in the air. He dragged the palm of his hand up and down his face, allowing himself a moment to acclimatise, attempting to get his head in gear. His arms were starting to feel detached from his body with fatigue. The dips in the road had given him a floaty feeling, reminiscent of the after-effects of childhood bouncy castles. He needed a lie-down, but there were practicalities to address and he wanted to get this induction over with. The sooner he was on his way back to the city, the better.

Wilcox hopped out of his truck and beckoned Sullivan to follow him towards the Town Hall.

'Welcome to the heart of West Galmore,' Wilcox unclipped a large ring of keys from his belt, 'Or as I call it, "home".'

Sullivan's eyes narrowed, but he tried to mask his displeasure by shielding his brow from the sun. Of course he knew that Wilcox lived in the town, its only resident for the past 20 years, but he had assumed he lived in one of the original resident shacks, not the largest building in town. That would soon have to change.

Wilcox fiddled with a padlock on the old door and pushed through to a dark hallway. Sullivan urged his fatigued body to follow through to the lobby. Cracked, peeling maroon paint and a moth-eaten rug greeted him; more things for the list. He cast his gaze around the dank room and sensed a shadow shift in his periphery. He twitched his head to the side, swung around, but saw nothing moving. A small noise of question slipped from his mouth, but his guide was already onto the next room. He dug his knuckles into his itchy tear ducts and prayed that Wilcox had prepared somewhere for him to sleep.

'I've left your keys on the front desk,' Wilcox called back to him, 'I'll have to show you which is which mind.'

'Let's just do the essentials now and a proper tour tomorrow.' Sullivan said, ducking under a garland of straggly clothes hanging from a length of rope. The place was a mess. He wondered whether his cleaner would travel from Denver for a week or two, tidy it up a bit before they started the renovations. Clearly, Wilcox had not been upholding his post as caretaker in the literal sense.

'Through here's the saloon,' Wilcox strode ahead. 'Not well stocked, but we have the essentials.' He croaked a dry chuckle and patted the bar as he passed.

Sullivan clocked the inventory lining the shelves: twenty or so identical bottles of cheap, bland whiskey. He wondered what sort of drinker Wilcox was, alone in the desert with all the time in the world.

'The infamous blackjack room.' Wilcox nodded to a small alcove leading off from the main corridor. Another of the listing's highlights. Sullivan leaned in to see the famous gunshot hole in the wall and heavy blood-stain beneath. That would need preserving under perspex before visitors started touching everything, devaluing everything. Then he noticed another dark patch on the floor, one that appeared to quiver. He held his breath for a moment, listening intently; yes, definitely a hum. He approached and crouched down, shuddering as the mass came into focus. Hundreds of bees were crawling out of the floorboards, some dead and some writhing in sticky groups. He snapped back to standing as fast as his knees would allow.

'What's with the bees?' He shouted, trying to keep his voice steady above the mix of disgust and annoyance he felt.

'On my to-do list. There's a nest of them in the walls. That's the problem with this old wood, it gets so dry out here that it's easy for bugs to bore their way in. You should have seen the locusts in '99.'

Sullivan pursed his lips. What exactly had this man been doing with his time for two decades?

'That's the old kitchen,' Wilcox continued on, pointing to a door on the far wall. 'More of a pantry to be frank. As you know, there's no running water and the cooker is long dead.'

Another problem that Sullivan had to figure out before any money could be made from the place. They couldn't expect guests to trek miles into the desert without providing some basic necessities. His selling point to the investors was advertising tours for "24 hours in a ghost town", a plan that capitalised on the novelty of the town without expecting much in the way of comfort. If you set expectations to live "like the original residents" then you didn't have to add any luxuries.

Wilcox didn't offer to show Sullivan his food supplies, which he imagined to be a stockpile of canned goods. But then he remembered the shotgun and tried not to envision carcasses spread out on the counter-tops.

'Bedrooms are up here.' Wilcox jangled his ring of keys as they climbed up the steep, wooden staircase and onto a landing flanked by two doors. 'I sleep here,' Wilcox said, knocking on one door, 'so you can stay in the other room tonight.'

Sullivan opened the door to a sparsely furnished room; a four-poster bed and dark pine wardrobe. He was surprised by the lack of clutter compared to the rest of the building.

'Don't you use this room?' He asked, relieved that not everywhere had succumbed to Wilcox's inhabitation.

'Oh hell no, that's the kids' room. Y'know, the kids that were locked in the closet and left to die.'

'Excuse me?' Sullivan exclaimed.

'Yeah, one of the *less marketable* ghost stories about this town I guess.' Wilcox scratched at his grey stubble. 'Most of them don't bother me, but shit I am not risking it with that creepy room. I'd take murderous prospector over neglected child any day.' He laughed to punctuate the sentence, but it was a humourless sound.

'Great', Sullivan breathed, and offloaded his bag onto the bed. He'd been dying for a nap all morning but this winded his enthusiasm. 'Well, I'm going to rest my eyes for a while.' Sullivan said, closing the door on Wilcox's back. The man was already heading back downstairs. Clearly, living alone for so long had eroded his social niceties.

Sullivan eyed the closet. Even though he felt on the brink of collapse, there was no way he'd be able to sleep until he'd checked inside. He felt childish as he approached and tentatively prised one of the doors open. A strong, musty smell seeped out as the door creaked towards him. The space was empty, no clothes, boxes, hangers or skeletons; he released his breath. But as he started to close the door, he caught sight of something on the floor of the closet.

'Oh what the hell.' Sullivan recoiled instinctively, then forced himself to take another look.

The dark wood was squirming. He bent closer and sighed as he recognised the twitching pattern of movement: woodworm. More rot. The investors wouldn't be happy about this. They'd question why he hadn't found it on his initial viewing of the property a few months back. He wouldn't be able to explain how his visit had been a swift one after hours, that he'd been nursing a hangover from a long night at the poker table. His first mistake had been to allow himself a stopover on the drive; his second had been the city of choice: Las Vegas. He'd got a cheap deal on a swanky hotel, promised himself there wouldn't be any time for gambling, but the temptation to hit the tables at the hotel's casino overpowered him. Then drinks kept arriving at his side, and soon he was in the zone, bluffing his way through the bad and the good. By 5am, he had doubled his deposit. Unfortunately, this meant Sullivan overslept his wakeup alarm, missed his viewing slot with the realtor and had to negotiate another opportunity later in the day, after everybody else.

When he found out that there was already a bid on the property, the value skyrocketed. If someone else wanted it, it must be worth the investment. His fresh winnings didn't burn a hole in his pocket for very long.

Now recalling his urgency to snap up the deal, he felt queasy. He thought he had an eye for a good investment, but his conviction was slipping away the longer he spent in the town. Tomorrow he would undertake a full assessment, do his due diligence and assess the damage. But right now, he didn't have the energy. He lay on the bed fully clothed, and the toll of the drive caught up with him. In two deep breaths he was in a deep, heavy sleep.

◆

When Sullivan woke, it was dark, and his hands and face were rigid with cold. He lay in the dreamy weight of half-sleep for a while longer, debating whether to slip back into the lull. But then a long creak of floorboards pulled him into consciousness. That feeling was back, of something in his periphery. He sat bolt upright and looked around. The room was dark, but the moon cast strips of light across the floor. It was silent again, and Sullivan assured himself that the creaking was normal; old buildings like this settled in the night. He'd just have to get used to such nuances. But just as he lay back onto the pillow, there was another squeak of floorboards near to the closet. He jumped out of bed, knocking his bag onto the floor. His skin prickled as he remembered Wilcox's story about the kids in the closet and he swiped at the wall near the door for a light switch before remembering that there was no electricity.

'Shiiiit,' he whispered into the silence. His voice was shaky, which increased his panic. He took his phone from his pocket and flipped on the torch setting, scanning the room quickly with its unnaturally white light. Nothing. The phone eked the miserable sound of a low battery and he quickly shut off the torch. His power bank was still in the car, that was a good enough reason to get out of the room, retrieve power and reassure himself with access to the modern world. He unpacked his duffle coat and pulled it around his stiff shoulders.

Downstairs, he found Wilcox sat in one of the booths in the saloon. He was bundled up in thick, grubby layers, illuminated in the shadows by a melting trunk of a candle. One of the whiskey bottles sat on the table, his thick hand gripping an empty tumbler next to it.

'Good sleep?' He asked as Sullivan collected himself a glass from the bar and slid into the booth.

'For the most part.' Sullivan replied, pouring himself two fingers of whiskey. Wilcox raised his brows as the whole glass went down in one swallow.

Sullivan smacked his lips, 'That doesn't go down without a fight does it?'

'More of a medication than a delectation. The nights here can be hard going.'

'Why do you stay then?' A question that Sullivan had wanted to ask since he'd found out about his residency.

'Cheap rent, quiet neighbours.' He laughed again. 'And of course the prospect of infinite wealth. Same reason prospectors came all the way out here originally.'

Two more glasses were poured and downed without discussion.

'Yeah but the mines were run dry hundreds of years ago.' Sullivan started to worry that the old man was even more delusional than he thought. The candle-light flickered across his eyes as he leaned in.

'Except for the lost silver vein.' His breath clouded in the cold air.

'I'm fairly sure that's a myth.' Sullivan countered, frank with his derision.

'Of course you think it's a myth. Otherwise *every* Tom, Dick and Harry would be up here with their fancy machinery wouldn't they. Those goddam sneaky bastards trying to steal what I earned.' His eyes darkened.

'Right.' There was condescension in Sullivan's voice, but he couldn't help wondering whether there was a glimmer of truth in Wilcox's statement, paranoid delusions aside. It was a tantalising prospect given that he legally owned the land, therefore technically also owned any potential silver lurking in the mines. He topped up their glasses.

'You'll have to show me where you think this vein might be.'

Wilcox chuckled, 'Somehow I don't see you down a mine.'

They downed their drinks. The whiskey was setting an unspoken bar of power that each nudged higher with every shot.

'Well sure, I want to see everything that I bought.' Sullivan tried to sound cool but flushed from the neck up with his obvious bid for control. He was grateful for the dark.

'I bet you ten bucks that you take one look down the mine shaft and run for the hills.'

'You're on.' They shook hands, firmly, soft and calloused together.

'Come on then, I'll show you.' Wilcox stood and leaned to grab the bottle but knocked it and the remainder of the whiskey across the table. 'Ah shit! Well it's a good job we drank most of it up already.'

Sullivan was also feeling the buzz of alcohol, but the idea of poking around mines in the middle of the night terrified him. 'We can't go now. It's god knows what time,' he said, pushing back in his chair to avoid the pool of liquor that was trickling over the edge of the table.

'Don't panic yourself,' Wilcox said with a note of scorn, 'I'm not taking you down the mine, just to the hoist house. The view from up there is incredible. We might even catch the sunrise. Unless you want to head back to your room…'

Sullivan thought of the eerie closet in the cold, dark room. Waiting until sunrise before revisiting that place sounded appealing.

'Sure, let's see what this town is made of.' Sullivan stood with such gusto that the table wobbled, the candle spitting wax across the wood. They both pretended not to notice and made their way out of the saloon into the crisp desert air.

'It's just about ten minutes up this road.' Wilcox said, climbing into his truck.

'You can't drive, you're drunk.' Sullivan said.

'Tipsy.' He corrected firmly. 'And of course I can drive, there's no one else on the road is there? Besides, we'd freeze hauling our asses up that dirt road.'

There was something irresistibly challenging about Wilcox's confidence, and Sullivan found himself opening the passenger door. To be fair to him, Wilcox was a fast but steady drunk driver. Sullivan imagined him sauced to the boots driving around the desert at speed. God help anyone who encountered him out on the real roads. As promised, they bounced all the way up the dirt road in under ten minutes. High up on a tussock tufted hillside, the hoist house was a ramshackle marvel. Sullivan had seen photos, but they didn't do it justice. It was huge compared to other buildings in the town, a large warehouse built from corrugated metal but missing whole walls and windows. They could see straight through to the structural innards.

Wilcox led the way inside, flashlight in hand, and Sullivan hastened to keep up with the light. His heart pounded with the prospects of childish dares.

'We should keep it brief in here.' Sullivan said, eying the

sagging ceiling. 'The place looks one windy night away from collapse.'

Wilcox let out his condescending chuckle, 'The desert storms have battered this place for decades and it still stands true. Check out this beauty.'

Wilcox shone the flashlight across wooden beams supporting a massive, intricate pulley system. He illuminated the machinery, casting the light down until a metal cage came into view, floating above an ominously dark gap in the floor.

'There's your mine-shaft entrance. Thirteen hundred feet down in that little cage. How'd you feel about that?'

Sullivan could imagine nothing worse than tackling that black descent, but felt a certain level of pride had to be maintained. Time to turn on the businessman charm. He forced a chuckle.

'Well, it's not my ideal day out but I'd love to see just what the fuss is all about.' There was no way he'd ever be going down the mine, but Wilcox probably wouldn't be around to see whether or not that happened.

'Well if you want something to sober you up I recommend a lung full of underground air.' Wilcox strode over to the cage and knelt on one knee, inhaling dramatically. The obvious muscle-flexing was starting to grind Sullivan's gears. 'Just don't drop your fancy telephone down the slats, you'll never see it again.'

Sullivan tightened the grip on his cell instinctively. He took reassurance in its presence; his lifeline to the real world. He resisted turning on the torch function despite feeling skittish that Wilcox controlled the light. Instead, he checked the time.

'Looks like we might be bang on time for sunrise.' Sullivan said, relieved to have an excuse to leave.

Outside, the sun was creeping up above the mountains, casting a warm glow over the valley and into the town. It was breathtaking. They stood in silence for a moment, appreciating the view, until Wilcox shouted, 'What the hell?' And shielded his eyes against the sun.

Sullivan followed his gaze and saw what Wilcox was looking at. 'Oh shit! The Town Hall is on fire!'

Wilcox strung a list of expletives together as he jogged back to his truck. 'We need to contain it, quickly. The whole town is bone dry timber.'

Sullivan followed suit, his shirt sticking to his back as he slid into the Cruiser. 'How much water do we have?' He asked, feeling winded.

'We're down to the last few gallons. Delivery is tomorrow.'

'I'll call the fire department in Deanwood.' Sullivan said, fumbling with buttons on his non-responsive phone, 'The goddamn battery's dead!'

But Wilcox wasn't listening. He was twisted round in his seat, swinging the truck back onto the road. They sped back to town at a sickening pace, and Wilcox pulled up so close to the blaze that the heat was palpable. Sullivan covered his mouth with his coat and squinted into the flames, his eyes burning from the smoke. His stomach dropped as he realised that the fire was already licking the adjacent building.

'Let's drive to Deanwood and get help.' He shouted over the sound of wood crackling, sweat beading on his temples. But Wilcox sat transfixed, his eyes on the Town Hall, his whole world aflame.

'Wilcox!' Sullivan grabbed the man by his arm and leaned close. 'We have to go. Now!'

'There's nothing we can do,' Wilcox muttered, 'Those goddam sneaky bastards just love to watch the world burn.' ◆

"I missed writing letters. I felt like a letter myself, written in the finest script and the most exquisite language, but not properly addressed."

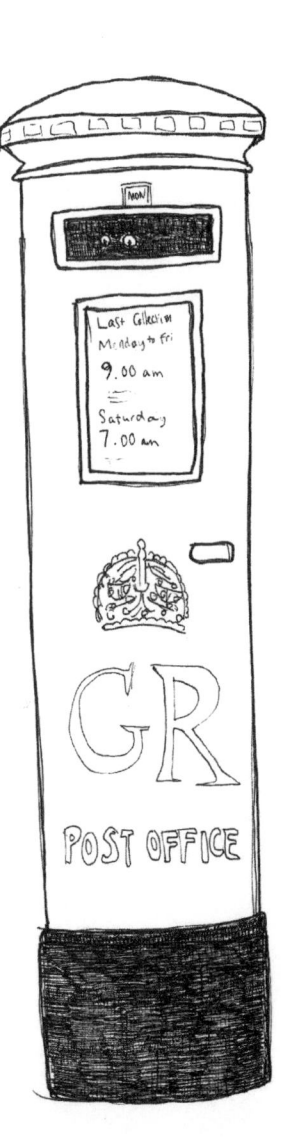

Collection

Neil James Hudson

◆

This city is full of vantage points. Windows punctuate buildings, eyes in the wall where an observer can hide behind a curtain, peek from a corner or even stand in full view, knowing no one would dare look through the window in return. High roofs provide platforms where anyone can lie and stare down at their quarry. The deep alleyways provide lurking space for the determined voyeur, as well as an escape route in the event of discovery. A thousand people wander the street, all showing some kind of purpose or activity, all of which could be faked. And couldn't the street furniture itself be surveillance equipment of sorts? The posts that support road signs could be vast periscopes operated by subterranean observers. Telephone junction boxes provide space to hide in, or to leave recording equipment to look at later. Even the post boxes, stationed around the streets like red sentries, could contain a devoted watcher, staring out through their single slot.

Knowledge is always stronger than reason, logic or evidence. When one knows one is being observed, one does not need to look for proof. One only needs to find the observer. I had not proven it was the postboxes - in fact, I felt that the drains and grilles in the street were a more fruitful line of enquiry - but my feeling of being watched, never absent, became a certainty when I passed in front of their black slots. I felt more solid, as if their invisible gaze gave me my existence. Large stand-alone boxes could house even someone of my size, while the boxes embedded in the walls could have small rooms behind them. I watched the post collectors visit their boxes, unlocking them with small keys. I wondered if the messages they removed were about me, or if I were merely an irritation who kept getting in the way, like a floater in the eye's surface.

I soon recognised all the post collectors and learnt their rounds, and they grew to recognise me. We never spoke, but they would briefly catch my eye with a look of recognition that seemed to see more of me than I saw in my own reflection. I watched them empty the boxes, trying to catch a glimpse of the person within. But they hid the boxes with their bodies, and I never saw if they were emptying them or making deliveries, providing the occupant with food, useful items or even letters.

I wondered about their relationship with their charges - that of jailers to the jailed, perhaps, or carers to their wards? They travelled the city freely, men and women to whom nowhere was closed. I watched one in particular, a woman with long blonde hair in a plait that seemed glued to her back like fins. She walked around with a cheerful expression, except when she glanced at me. Then she seemed to acknowledge me, not as a comrade exactly but as someone whose life intertwined with hers. As a doctor looks at a patient, when the doctor knows the patient's fate, but the patient does not.

I approached one of her boxes after she had left it. The look she had given me as she left seemed to be an invitation, permission to look closer. It was not a box in itself, merely a facade that hovered in the wall of a shop. Its slot peered back at me as I squinted through, wishing I'd brought a torch, but I saw nothing. I wondered if the boxes were sentient, and had no occupant. Perhaps the post collectors delivered sustenance, which they placed directly into the box's stomach. I touched its red armour, hoping I could elicit a reaction, then took my hand away. I wasn't sure if my act had been aggressive or invited closer intimacy, and I wondered if I should apologise.

'Who's there?' I said finally, speaking into the slot. 'Who's in there? What are you doing?'

But all I heard was the sound of someone holding their breath.

◆

It was a mistake, of course. There is only one way to communicate with a postbox, and that is by letter. Not many people write them any more, the biggest clue to their change of use. Whatever the post collectors were doing at the boxes, it wasn't collecting post.

I missed writing letters. I felt like a letter myself, written in the finest script and the most exquisite language, but not properly addressed. I had never found my recipient. I set to my task with gusto. There were so many questions I wanted answering. How had they come to be inside the postbox - was it a fate they had chosen, or had they been press-ganged by the collectors? What was it in their earlier life that had suited them to this existence? What did they look at, and what did they think of it? I wanted to tell them about myself, about how I had spent my life hiding in the shadows; of how as a child, I would sit and deliberately try to take in the entire scene in front of me and consciously take note of every discrete item in my vision - each nuance and shade of colour, howling in frustration when I became aware of yet another detail that I had not noticed.

By the evening's end, I saw that I had written three words - "I am ready."

I sealed them in an envelope and did not write an address. The next morning, I went to the postbox and pushed it through the slot gently, so as not to harm the person inside.

◆

I was collected the next week. At first I wondered if she was going to put me in a sack, haul me over her shoulder and carry me off, to squeeze me through the slot on arrival at my box. But in fact she looked at me, the smile gone, and nodded once. She locked the box she was visiting, then turned and walked towards her van. The passenger door of her van was already open, and I climbed in silently. As we drove, I had a brief fantasy that I was the collector, promoted to the ranks of the privileged. But the daydream was as short as the journey.

It was a double box, with two slots, large, standing out in the pavement. People walked past it without noticing, despite its solidity and bright red appearance. My collector unlocked the left-hand side.

The panel seemed too small for me to pass through, but she stood back and watched me, and it was clear that the time for changing my mind was in the past. First I tried to push my head in, then I decided to go in feet first. I was surprised that the base of the box was below ground level and I landed painfully. I pulled the rest of my body in and turned around. As I'd hoped, my eyes were at the level of the slot.

She turned the key in the lock, and I watched her depart on the rest of her rounds. Then I began to watch the street, finally having time to take in every last detail, unseen in return.

◆

I still do not know if she is my jailer or my carer. She visits me twice a day, dropping off supplies. The day I ask to be let out has not come and will not do so for some time. When it does, I will find out.

But I do know why I am here.

This box was built for holding people, not mail. That came later. The floor is a metal grille which allows for the disposal of waste into the sewers. It is comfortable to live in. A metal wall divides the two halves, and as far as I can tell, the other side is empty.

I found my recruit after only a couple of weeks. A girl, not long out of her teens, who always walked with her head down, as if to hide her face. But I took in enough of it as I watched her. Her hair was naturally wavy, as I knew she would not call attention to herself by having it treated, and she wore only enough make-up to pass unnoticed. She hunched her shoulders as if they were a protective carapace. I was often chastised for wearing the same posture when I was in my teens.

There was no need to make contact. Everyone knows when they're being watched. I simply fixed my gaze on her whenever she came past, knowing that she knew, waiting for her own curiosity to do the work for me. And it wasn't long before I was rewarded. I could hardly contain my excitement as I saw her approach the box with determination. I looked at her eyes as she peered through the slot, knowing she would not see anything in the darkness. She spoke softly. 'Is there… is there someone in there?'

I held my breath. There was no need to say anything. Her letter would come soon. The box beside me was ready, and all that was needed was for the collector to let her in, so we would look out over the street together, studying its every detail, guarding it from the humiliation of not being seen.♦

Galaxies

Laura Turner

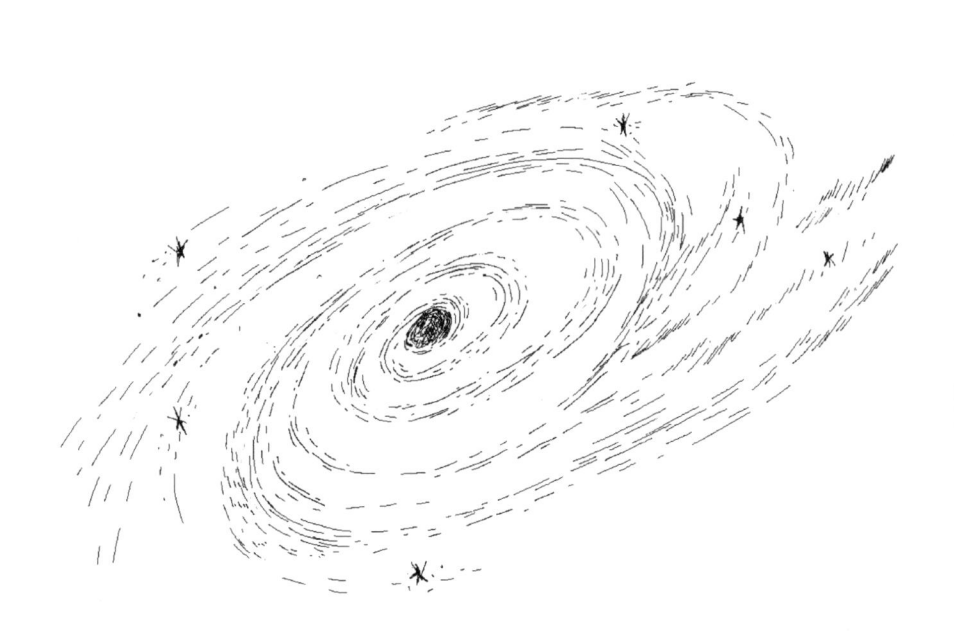

◆

I've ached like stars across the galaxies
torn from sisters, snatched to another place,
empty cold land, frontiers they never sought.
Branches wrenched adrift across the mud-locked marsh.
We look for friends, air to breathe: gravity.
But when none comes - what then?
What tethers us, what keeps me, me?
You are you, but what if I can't do that?
I can't be like you. I'm lost. Alone.
A galaxy apart and empty spaces,
all that's left.◆

"And so, when they'd said goodbye, and he'd closed the door behind her, the sense of loss flooded in again like a sudden tide."

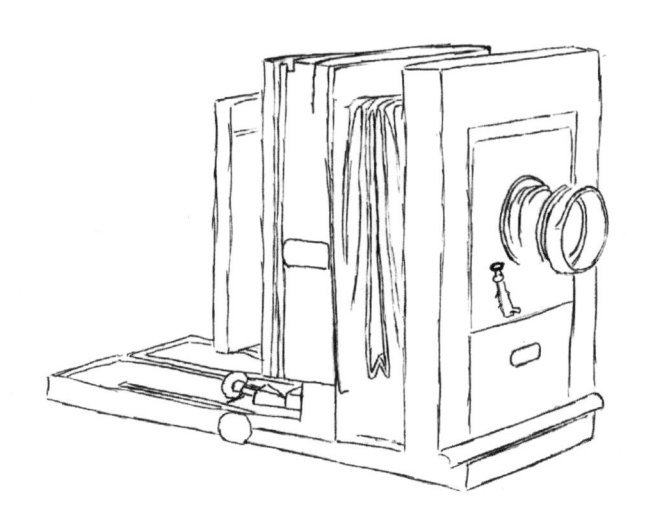

Leaving May

Robert Powell

◆

May returned to him in the Spring of 1985, when he was seventy-six. Since losing her two decades before, he had lived on reluctantly, a virtual hermit in their Georgian townhouse on the faded street at the end of which the cathedral stood in its quarry full of graves, like a ship in eternal dry-dock. In this once-great port city he had been master of the most sought-after portrait studio, the one to whom had flocked the civic great and good, lesser royalty, actors and music hall celebrities, opera singers and film stars, all here to parade on the stage of the Grand Theatre, lay foundation stones and launch ships. They had stood in his studio before the cyclops eye of his camera, and later, all had received their meticulously retouched likenesses. On the back of each was a pasted label depicting a classical Roman girl, robed in white and seated by a pool with a fawn at her feet. Below her were the words:
Winston and Wutherall, Photographers

In the early days, each image had borne the signatures of both partners. They'd met in the army, on the North-West Frontier. He, Wutherall, was the obsessive one even then, standing frozen in the heat and smoke of the hill villages, holding his breath while the camera recorded the natives, their houses and temples. Then processing the images by night, in the suffocating tent, without electricity, and with huge moths flapping in to explode the lamps in the spirit-fuelled enlarger. Winston, also a photographer but with a "damn good head for figures", looked on admiringly. After a couple of years, they decided to get out and, financed entirely by Winston's money, they set up their business in the city that was Winston's home.

The city then was in its prime, bustling with trade, and slowly but surely the studio began to thrive. Then, one Saturday morning in their third trading year, waiting for a late client and watching the drizzle fall lazily into the street beyond the studio window, Winston collapsed and died. Wutherall was left, singular. But their double-barrelled brand, with its assonance and repetition, was already rooted, and so he kept it. Now, however, at the bottom of the photographs, only his signature appeared: *Edward Wutherall*. And there was another change too, a new word after his name: *Artist*.

Yet his clients still received double value, for she was already there. May Christabel Hunter was an able and handsome girl from the middling leafy suburbs on the far side of the river, who they'd hired as an assistant as soon as the accounts had started to show a profit. She came in early every morning, managed the diary, did the book-keeping, ordered the chemicals, fresh flowers, props and backdrops, kept the proliferating array of equipment in order. She instructed the staff, welcomed the sitters, catalogued and filed the hundreds and then thousands of negatives and prints, and she loved him.

They married in the cathedral (the bishop was a client) in June of 1930. From then on they did everything together. In 1938, with the business booming, they moved the studio and themselves to the grand house they'd bought among the doctors and solicitors in the fashionable Georgian terrace that overlooked the city. Fixed to pillars on either side of the large, pale green door, decorative plaques proclaimed: *Winston & Wutherall - Sittings by Appointment*. From cellar to roof, the house had two dozen rooms, and each was in use: offices, the darkroom, fixing room, storage, finishing, and retouching. At its height, seven staff were engaged, working from eight in the morning until six at night. Clients would be formally received and seated in the large front Waiting Salon, then transferred to the Changing Room to don the suits and dresses and accessories they were offered or had brought. Then May would lead them, with due solemnity, up the stairs to The Studio, with its drawn theatre curtains, huge lamps on stands, dais, pillars, screens, and of course, the camera.

On some Wednesday afternoons during half-day closing, and certainly on Sundays, they loaded cameras and picnic hamper, and drove into the countryside to pursue Wutherall's main creative passion, landscape. For holidays, they sought out mountains, enjoying the way the light and the weather changed quickly, pouring giddily around them, sculpting and re-sculpting the visible world. He saw it as his artistic mission to locate the very essence of that haste, catch it, and halt it.

After the War, the studio remained successful, at least for a while. Then, in shifting times, the generations of the Twenties and Thirties gradually faded away, and with them their business. On his birthday, in the late autumn of 1965, Wutherall officially retired, and he and May began to plot the great "Photographic Odyssey" they would make together the following spring. They would go to Northern Europe, the Mediterranean, Africa, and eventually back to his old haunts in India.

On Christmas Day that year, it snowed heavily in the morning, stopping around noon. At two, he returned to their drawing room, with tea. The room was unusually bright, filled by the outstretching reflection of the whiteness that lay everywhere outside. And in this splendid light, May sat in the armchair beneath his favourite portrait of her, completely paralysed. She died in St. Lucy's Hospital two days later.

During the first week, he was mystified. That May wasn't here with him was not possible. It was unacceptable. He needed her advice. Which funeral director should they use? Who should they invite? What refreshments should they serve?

After the funeral, he simply became aware of a new blandness - in the house, in the streets, in the world. At first, he fought it, using what was left of her that he could touch. He set about gathering her material life and going through everything that had been hers, her books and letters, her phonograph collection, her dresses, hats, and stockings. Every last thing. Holding these objects in his hands, he managed for a while to paper over the gaping hole of her absence. By means of his upbringing, his military training, and sheer habit, he kept the mechanics of life in motion. He went out, bought the *Daily Chronicle* and the *British Journal of Photography*, ate and slept. He turned the ground floor changing room into a bedroom and barely ventured into the rest of the house, and certainly not up to the studio.

Only the drawing room, with its portrait of May, retained any pretence of normality. Here, he read or gazed blankly out of the window at the crumbling terrace opposite. Above and below this one space, along the hallways, in the cellars, up the carpeted stairs, through the studio; in room after room, the house lay in dust.

◆

May came back to him twenty years later. She was in the company of a young curator who was researching an exhibition. On that first visit, she sat under her own portrait. She was now a more talkative woman, less self-effacing than she had been before. It was understandable, he supposed, that she would take on this more modern personality, that her demeanour and attitude would be those of a young woman whose girlhood had been shaped by all the silliness that had gone on in the 1960s and 70s. Her body was different too, her hair lighter, the lines on either side of her mouth more pronounced when she smiled. And of course, they had given her another name.

'Janet…' she said, smiling and reaching to take his hand. 'Janet Talbot.'

Yet he had no doubt that she was May. Her eyes were May's, as were her alert eyebrows that lifted inquisitively when something interested her, animating her face with an expression that was an intriguing mixture of enthusiasm and interrogation. When he took his eyes from her, reluctantly, to speak to the curator, he felt May's presence in the room, here with him after these many years. When he left her briefly on that first visit to search for a book, he could feel how the house responded to her. It lightened and sharpened, became more vivid, like a mountain landscape emerging from mist.

And so, when they'd said goodbye, and he'd closed the door behind her, the sense of loss flooded in again like a sudden tide. It overwhelmed him. He sat in the gloom on the hallway stairs, letting his cane slip to the floor, and wept. It was as if she had died again.

As he sat there, however, his grief was slowly replaced by something else. It was the kind of exhilaration that he'd felt when they were together in the mountains, on the verge of discovering a view that he knew would make a successful artwork.

She wasn't dead. She was back in the world, and he was no longer alone.

'Janet Talbot, Janet Talbot,' he whispered to the empty hallway. 'Janet Talbot…'

He retrieved his cane from the floor, shuffled into the drawing room, and picked up the business card the curator had left. He sat down at the writing desk and composed a letter on his headed notepaper, *Winston & Wutherall*, expressing "enthusiasm for the proposed exhibition project" and offering an unprecedented degree of access to his work, his house, himself. And at the very end of the note, as though an afterthought, he wrote "how wonderful it had been, and would be again" to have "your delightful companion" with them on "this exciting venture". He slipped into the envelope one of the original labels she had admired, with the Roman girl, the pool, and the fawn… "For Miss Talbot".

There then began a series of curatorial visits, a series he prolonged through the careful control of information. He revealed his work and his memories with gradually-portioned tidbits, and always made sure to finish each meeting with something that would tantalise and necessitate another. Of course, he had to learn to disguise his disappointment (and curtail the session) when the tedious young man arrived without May. Once he discovered the overall pattern of her availability, he manipulated his empty diary to schedule sessions on those days. He also began to nurture not just a "professional" relationship focused on the exhibition, but a personal one: one that would, he hoped, encourage them to visit him as his friends, even if together.

The craft, although unnatural to him, worked. She came, and again the drawing room of the old house was transformed into a warm, convivial place of conversation, even laughter. At first, she was just in attendance, mainly listening, looking and making notes, but increasingly, she played a more active role, even adding her own questions to those of her, her what? Companion? Lover? Boyfriend?

'Oh, we're just friends,' she laughed. But he noticed her shared glance with the curator.

◆

One day near midsummer, leaving the curator to go through several boxes of negatives, he took her on a tour of the house, hoping it would stir something in her; a recollection, a memory.

When it was over, and they went through the back door and into the long, overgrown garden, she was enthralled. 'What a wonderful place!' she cried in undisguised delight. Not surprising, he thought, since she had planned, planted, and then nurtured it for almost thirty years.

It was in a sad state now, though. Aside from a small area of flagstones near the house, with the stone bench that he sometimes still sat on, it had gone to wrack and ruin. Dark, thick tangles of weeds and brambles covered the path to the greenhouse and the collapsing garage, beside which an Anderson shelter sat strangled in ivy.

In the city, the bells of the cathedral sounded the hours of noon. It had been raining, but now the sun appeared. May offered to prune some of the roses that hung down, glistening bright and wet. Fumbling in the wreckage of the potting shed, he found her a pair of half-rusted secateurs, and she set to work. He wiped the rain off of the bench with his handkerchief and sat leaning on his cane, watching.

It was wonderful to see her move, to see her turn and smile at him, young flesh against the corroding brick of the high walls. For the first time in years, he longed for his camera. He could catch this moment. He could keep it, and keep her.

'Anyone for tea?' said the curator from the doorway.

He convinced himself that what he longed for most was simply her companionship. But in bed, half-asleep, he imagined her body. He saw her crouched in the garden at dusk, naked, a living sculpture, with her knees drawn up to her chin and her arms around them. He sat up, awake and ashamed.

Yet was she not cooperating? He saw that she felt safe in his presence. She flirted. She was careless. During visits she now always sat next to him on the sofa. She found excuses to follow him to the cluttered kitchen, or here and there in the house as he went to find a file or a book. One warm July day, although it remained chilly in the house, she arrived wearing shorts and a loose blouse that exposed her tanned arms. And, for the first time, she came alone.

'Oh, I just fancied your company!' she smiled, heading to the kitchen to make tea. His heart beat quickly, with a delightful pain.

But how, as the summer went by, was he ever to establish a completely separate relationship with her and be rid of her "friend"? How to contrive to have her to himself, where she would be *her true self* again?

◆

A way was found.

In fact the idea had come to them both at precisely the same instant. One afternoon when the three of them were sitting together in the now-rejuvenated garden, the curator handed him a book on Cecil Beaton that he'd brought along to illustrate some point about studio lighting. Taking it, he noticed her name written inside the cover.

'Ah,' he said, looking up at her, 'this is yours?'

'Yes. It's Beaton's fashion work I'm interested in. My final dissertation was on fashion.'

'Your dissertation?'

'Yes, it was for my degree. On the period between the First World War and the Second, and how it affected fashion in the Sixties. Carnaby Street...'

'Carnaby Street?'

'Yes, you know, Mary Quant, Twiggy, and all that.'

'Ah yes. Of course. Mary Quant...'

'I'd really like to go on to do an M.A, now. Just on women's fashion this time. I've been looking around for a topic...'

He started to say, 'Well, why don't you have a look at my...' And simultaneously she began 'Do you think, maybe...'

For what was the main part of his life's work: thousands of portraits of the ghosts of men and women from the 1930s, 40s and 50s, lying in their best costumes in their boxes in the dust, in rooms stacked with his negatives and file-prints, what were they, if not an entirely unexplored archive of women's tastes and trends from those years?

And so it was decided, there and then. Where her curator-friend was interested in his landscape and documentary work, she would focus her research on the element of his portraits: *Gender and Class in English Provincial Fashion, 1930-1960: The Studio Portraiture of Edward Wutherall.*

Now his direct path to her was open. She quickly obtained acceptance from the university, and they organised a series of sessions in which she would come to spend more time with him, alone.

To him, these days were like pearls on a necklace; wonderful illuminated things that gleamed through that autumn of 1985 when she came to the house and sat in the old Finishing Room, poring over negatives, prints, and studio records, and talking. Usually, he sat with her, pretending to guide her research, but in reality, he just watched.

She was finally here with him again. The house glowed. When they had finished for the day, she would make them tea, and they'd sit in the drawing room as they had done for so many years, over the Crown Ducal tea service, the light fading slowly in the windows and darkness falling.

It was perfect. Almost. For the young woman still hadn't realised that she was now where she belonged. She still believed that she was someone else. She didn't understand that she was May and had been returned to him, wearing a new body like a costume. She had travelled a long way. She had come back. But she hadn't yet realised that she was home. He needed to find a way to make her see. And then, of course, to keep her here for good.

◆

His plan was given further urgency by the arrival of an embossed envelope.

Mr and Mrs William Talbot have the pleasure of inviting you to attend the marriage of their daughter Catherine Janet…

She was going to be married, and to the curator! Why hadn't she told him? And it wasn't just the marriage: it was the fact, discovered on her next visit, that the proposal had been triggered by an invitation to the curator to become Director of an art gallery abroad. She was going to be taken far away from him.

On an afternoon when she'd finished her day's research and they sat together drinking tea, as she was enthusing about the dress worn in the 1936 full-length portrait of a Mrs J. S. Fisher, Wutherall posed his own question.

'How would you like it if I were to take your portrait in that same way?'

'*My* portrait?'

'Yes. I can make you look precisely like that woman, in that sort of setting, at that time.' He leaned forward, smiled, and touched her wrist.

'Perhaps as a wedding gift?'

Over the ensuing days, he set about the task like a demon. The challenge was daunting. Everything to do with the studio, so well organised by May, had been moved or neglected since she'd left.

He knew he had the right plates, somewhere. And wouldn't they simply be too old, their photosensitivity degraded? The chemicals for developing, for fixing, he could mix himself from powders, as he'd had to do in the old days. But where had he put them? The huge lights hadn't been used for perhaps thirty years, and they were heavy and ponderous. The Studio was a mess, all dust and debris, mouse droppings on the Persian carpet, curtains laced with mould. It took his cleaner, especially commissioned and complaining, three full days to clear it.

And then there was the camera. It had to be the huge Kodak Century 7 half-plate, with its three-inch brass lens and great wooden bellowed casing, supported on wrought-iron legs and wheels.

He couldn't stop himself. He didn't sleep. He moved about like an automaton and at a snail's pace. He exhausted himself carrying things upstairs and down. Despite this, he felt young again. The image of the studio as it had once been, with her in it, shimmered in his mind. He was convinced that through the portrait, and their making it together, that she would see. She would see.

The day arrived. He dressed formally, just as he used to do when the studio was in its heyday, when people expected *decorum* - dark suit, waistcoat, tie, the tie-pin and matching cufflinks May had given him for their tenth anniversary in 1940.

Foregoing breakfast and forgetting his daily pills, he paced in the drawing room, then up and down the hall. She was due at ten. This morning, out of necessity, he would take on the role that she had played all those years ago, greeting her, putting her at ease, taking her through the necessary stages. While he remained discreetly outside, she would try on various accoutrements, calling him in to inspect her and help her decide which to wear. They would choose her jewellery, shoes, handbag and wrap. Then she'd be ready to proceed up the stairs to the studio.

Although it was almost ten, he decided he would check just

one more time that everything was in order there. Nervously, he hauled himself upwards, cane in his left hand, bannister gripped with his right.

But it was all too slow, and he was still inspecting the camera when, simultaneously, the doorbell rang and the cathedral bells began to sound ten o'clock. He turned too quickly, fell onto his knees. He got up, steadied himself, gripping the great camera. He looked around the room, cave-like and darkened, so carefully reconstructed from the past. Resurrected.

The doorbell rang again.

May, he said, or thought.

He imagined her standing in the street, her beautiful face uplifted, at first smiling, then perplexed. The bell rang several times more, echoing up from the hall below. Then it went silent. A minute later - the time it took her to walk to the red phone-box on the corner - the black phone on the studio table jangled loudly, and its twin echoed up from downstairs.

Once, in the northwest of Ireland, they had driven together on an autumn afternoon into a valley they'd not seen before. The sky was full of vast cumulus clouds, but the late sun slanted down and filled the whole vista with an extraordinary burnished light. For a period, they seemed to float, suspended. In this strange, incalculable lapse of time, the car's interior felt like a transparent seed drifting in space, filled with watery gold. They'd stopped on the green verge, quickly unloaded the tripod, almost desperately, and set the Graflex pointing into that light to catch it before the vast rolling cliffs of cloud fell across the peaks, and everything changed and was lost.

Days later, back in the darkroom, he'd found that they'd caught nothing of value, nothing he could keep. But as they drove away down the curving mountain road, rain crackling on the car roof, May had reached over and touched his arm.

'Edward,' she'd said.

The phone rang again.

He stood beside his camera. Eyes closed, he saw her walking away from their house, along the faded street, past the cathedral with its empty quarry and graves, and back down into the busy, flowing city.◆

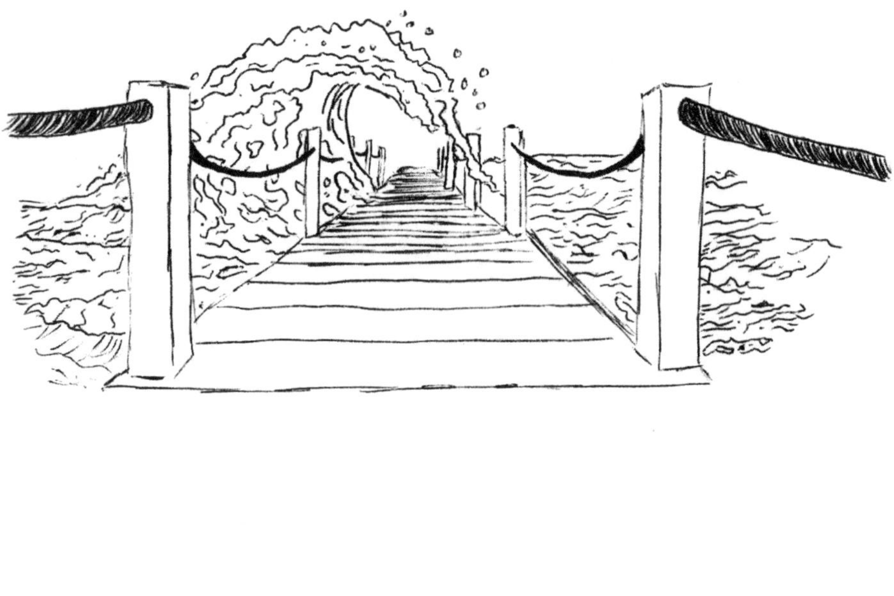

Beyond the Storm

Kitty Greenbrown

◆

I rang him from Peterhead,
4 o'clock in the morning.
Sea's raging I said -
I can't do this again.
It's okay he said,
We can be Rey and Kylo Ren.

I was on Saltburn Pier at 6
Spray stinging my face.
I've got that thing! I shout into WhatsApp -
Where I can't feel my hands!
It's alright he said,
Remember? We're Connell and Marianne.

At 10 I'm slipping on the cobbles in Staithes.
Sea's higher than ever, twice as fierce I say.
He doesn't falter.
We'll FaceTime until the wind subsides,
I'm Steve Rogers, you're Peggy Carter.

By lunch, I'm in Cornwall
Doubled up the rain.
It keeps cutting out! I shout.
Be Gidget, I'll be Max he says.

But I can't!

And he says,
You have a life raft, small sandwiches and something to read,
It's all you need.
Be Ponyo, I'll be Sosuke.

But I can't - I need you with me.

Well I won't be for a while,
And you don't.
He's quiet, I play for time
And what about when the storm breaks?
Who will we be then! I yell
That's easy love
Then, we'll be ourselves. ◆

"As I moved to take the glass and replace it with a seashell, he took hold of my wrist. I watched as the pale veins in his hand moved like the plump bodies of earthworms."

The Artist

Amy Farrar

◆

It was during the winter of 1997 that I decided to find the artist. He had become something of a myth in my town, the subject of whispers in the playground, a bogeyman whose tales fathers told to keep children firmly in their beds at night.

I only ever saw my father at the dinner table. When we'd finished eating, he would drop his thick hairy forearms on the wood, like two rabbits in rigor mortis, and light his cigar. One evening, after he had struck the match, I asked him what he knew about the artist. He released one long plume of smoke and said we don't discuss men like that in this house. I thanked him for the roast chicken and left the room as it stank of curdled butter and sweat.

The next day I walked the mile to the promenade where the arcades grew out from sea fret that lingered like bad breath. Seagulls loomed and screamed and fought over greasy polystyrene trays. Snow had melted into slurry. A metallic grey deluge from the boots of workers congealed against the entrances to *Treasure Island* and *Premier Amusements*. Men with beer guts and pink, calloused knuckles sat hunched over slot machines with their eyes half shut, glossy and weeping like the inside of a mouth. Lights, the colours of penny sweets, flashed with cries of canned laughter as a teenage boy whacked-a-mole with a worn pink hammer.

I rattled the coins in my coat pocket. It had become a habit to collect them after my father had fallen asleep in his leather armchair, jaw crooked and nails bitten to the intimate pink beneath. Silver and copper would slip into the cracks, and I would sneak down in the middle of the night to free them from the weary skin. Moving them around the violet flesh of my palm, I counted enough for a bag of doughnuts.

Kev's Doughnuts was a single booth between two grabber machines, each promising a prize every time. The stash of captive prizes was always the same: plush cartoon characters, goo-filled keyrings, pot woodland creatures or if you were especially lucky, a Nokia 3310. Kev stood behind the plastic counter, taught, spatula in hand, and watched the dough seeping from the machine with yellow eyes like two rotten onions found at the bottom of the fridge. His wrists were peppered with scars, and his nails were gummed up with flour and rancid grease.

I placed the coins on the counter and arranged them in order of size. Kev looked up from the machine as steam pooled from the rim.

'The usual?'

I nodded and pushed sugar crystals around the tower of coins to make a glittering moat.

'Kev?'

'Umhm.'

'What do y'know about the artist?'

'The artist? What yer wan' t'know about him for?'

'Just curious. Have you ever seen 'im?'

'O'course I 'ave. Not f'r years, mind.'

He slid his spatula into the oil and one by one, folded the fried dough into a vat of bleached white sugar. I saw a dead bluebottle mixed in with the grains. It had three legs and one split wing.

'Does 'e still live in that big 'ouse on'top've the cliff?'

'I havn't 'eard otherwise. He moved to America for a while in t' sixties an' seventies. Los Angeles, I believe. 'e were always in those posh magazines, y'know the ones. In't hairdressers and that. Queer sorta fella. Didn't much talk t'anyone round here. Thought 'e were too posh f' us I imagine.'

He said the word posh as if he were swallowing a teaspoon of cod liver oil.

'What does 'e look like?'

Kev shrugged his shoulders. 'You know...Posh. Queer. Rich. Always wore tweed, even in t' summer. Needed a haircut. Still always sounded Yorkshire, mind. No matter 'ow much 'e tried to 'ide it.'

The hairs in his nostrils quivered as he spoke. He sniffed and wiped his nose on the back of his hand. I tapped my fingers on the tin shelf and saw him add an extra doughnut into the striped paper bag. It left a grease stain in the shape of an oak leaf.

'America. 'ave you ever been?'

'Oh, I go all' time. Six days a week, eleven hours a day at this counter and the seventh day in Florida.'

He handed me the bag, and I felt the oil burn the pads of my fingers.

'Ta Kev.'

I followed the peeling red railing along the seafront and came too close to a group of skinny teenagers on bikes. The boys chewed on unlit cigarettes and the girls peered at me; the skin of their foreheads pulled tight into velvet scrunchies with too much gel. I picked a doughnut apart and let a piece scorch my tongue. The sugar melted and gave way to lumps of fat that slid down my throat and left a comforting weight under my ribs. One of the girls spat on the tarmac as I passed.

The tide was out, so I hopped down from the promenade and landed on a heap of brown sand that smelt of fish guts and dog shit. The wind whipped my hair around my skull, bringing with it tiny grains that stung my eyes and burnt my cheeks. My nose grew numb and I could taste the salty tang of snot mingled with sugar as I sucked it from my fingers.

A crow and a seagull fought over a lobster that was still alive. It was black and speckled, and the flesh that was being ripped from beneath its shell was plump and white like marshmallow. I stepped on the wet coils of sand that worms had left behind. My father had said you could dig for the worms and use them as bait, but I didn't want to bother them. I had told him they already had tough enough lives, being born as worms. He had looked past me and left the room, muttering under his breath and picking the grit out from under his fingernails with a pocket-knife.

Scrunching the paper bag into a ball, I rolled it between my palms and dropped it into my coat pocket. I accidentally stepped on a razor shell and it split apart under my boot. The shell had been as long as my hand and was riddled with pearlescent freckles and the dried husks of lichen. It had been beautiful. I thought shells would make a wonderful present for the artist. My father never liked beautiful things, and everyone said he was a decent lad. If everyone in my town thought decent people hated something as beautiful as a seashell, I was certain the artist would think otherwise.

I collected three common mussels, two prickly cockles, half a dozen limpets and best of all, a dog whelk with the slimy host still inside. I found a large crab claw that could still be manipulated into movement, its orange muscle still intact, but it stank of the juice that leaks from over-filled bin bags, so I buried it. I had found a great scallop shell, but it was broken and I didn't want to bring the artist anything that wasn't perfect, so I buried that too. I ran my fingers across the worn ridges and silky insides as they sat, waiting, deep in my pockets. My hair had begun to smell like rotten seaweed.

Leaving south beach and crossing the boundary into the north, I climbed over slippery rock formations and discarded fishing nets until I saw his house on the clifftop. It grew out from the earth, unnaturally smooth against the rugged white, like burnt skin that has scabbed and healed and no longer looked as though it belonged to the same body. Moss spilled over the sides and dripped into the chalk. A single puffin perched on a ledge. The shells rattled in my pocket. I wiped my nose on my sleeve.

As I approached the winding staircase, I wondered what I would say to him. The first few steps were steep and there was no railing. The wind whistled and drowned out all noise. All I could hear was my heartbeat as it hammered against the sinew in my neck. I blew on my fingers to warm them. A light spattering of hail landed on weeds either side of the stone, and I continued to climb. My thighs burned and I tried my best not to look down.

When I reached the top, I could see all the way to the next bay. I stood and watched it for a moment before turning and climbing over the garden wall. It wasn't particularly high. A broken piece of slate caught my palm and peeled away a slice of skin which landed in a little white curl like pith from a tangerine. There was no grass in his garden, only pebbles the colours of sugared almonds. They made a pleasing crunch under my boots. The back door was ajar. As I put my cheek against the door, I could smell burnt onions, boiled vegetables and the cloying perfume of roses close to death. We had roses at home before my mother left. They always smelt at their strongest just before they died, as if revealing their true selves in a last panicked attempt at life.

I slid through the gap. I was good at things like that. My limbs were skinny and I could move them at peculiar angles. My splayed fingers landed on a kitchen counter which was cluttered with letters yet to be opened. The room was thick with steam. Pans were bubbling on the stove, so I turned them all off. One which was filled with a viscous soup had already overflowed onto olive green tiles. I ran my finger through it and tasted parsnip.

'Peter? Peter, Is that you?'

I stepped back against the sink, my teeth bared.

'Peter? I dropped my pills, Peter. Can you see them? Damn these eyes.'

The kitchen opened up into a grand room with a wall made entirely of glass. The brown stretch of the north beach could be seen from this obscene window, even the lighthouse that stood miles away. Dog eared books were over-flowing from cases that reached up to the ceiling. Clusters of vases spread about the room with flowers in differing stages of vigour. The scent was unbearable.

The artist breathed heavily in his simple wooden chair. He was leaning toward the glass with his back to me, his arthritic hands working through the tufts of a sheepskin rug. His hair fell past his ears in loose white waves. A lilac shirt, at least two sizes too big, hung limply from his shoulders. There was an iron burn on the left shoulder.

'For goodness sake Peter, can you help me? What on earth am I paying you for?'

I walked toward the chair and kneeled in front of him. I looked up into his face. His eyes were like two marbles, bulging and milky with smears of red. There were two pink pills, the size of my little fingernails, sat together by his slippered foot. I picked them out from the rug and placed them into his warm hand. His skin was surprisingly soft. He smelt like expensive soap and black coffee.

'Pass me the glass, it's over there on the table.'

The pills rattled as they hit his back teeth. I found the glass beside two clay sculptures of severed heads and a fresh apple core. He reached his hands out, palms up, like the painting of the crucifixion that hung in my classroom. His face even had the same waxy yellow pallor. I gave him the water, and his hand trembled as he lifted it.

I walked around the room and ran my hands over his books and empty canvases. The cut on my hand left a tiny smear of blood on a copy of *Orlando*. I pulled the dead leaves from some lilting lilies, their pollen staining my skin, and tidied some half empty mugs into a straight line.

As I moved to take the glass and replace it with a seashell, he took hold of my wrist. I watched as the pale veins in his hand moved like the plump bodies of earthworms. His nostrils flared.

'You're not my Peter.'

I did not reply. The blank pearls of his eyes shuddered.

'You've come from the sea. I can smell it on yer.'

He released his grip and ran his fingers over the dog whelk as if it were a thing that could burn him. Petals of psoriasis bloomed in the crevices of his knuckles. As I looked down, I saw that the heel of my hand still bled, and a print of my blood had settled in the crease of his thumb.

'You've been to the sea too. In America.'

He sat up straighter and the deep crags in his forehead drooped. A seagull landed on the slate wall outside, tilted its head, and studied us through the window with the yellow bead of one eye.

'That I did, Lad. That I did, but the sea there wa'nt same.'

I placed three cockles into the palm of his other hand. His fingers closed around them like the legs of a dying crab.

'The colours of glass in the sand, it wa'nt the same, or the stink of the salt as it dries on yer skin. No, it were never the same.'

He searched for my hands and returned the shells to me as the seagull threw back its head and screamed.◆

Contributors.

Alicia V McClane
Alicia is an editor by day and a writer by night. She has worked in publishing for over seven years, but only recently started to submit fiction for publication. She loves writing stories that merge the bizarre with the everyday. Her current midnight writing project is a novel about an accidental cult.

Amy Farrar
Currently living in York, Amy holds a BA in Film Studies and has completed a course in creative writing, with a focus on the short story. Amy's long-term goal is to be able to write full time, and is currently working on her second novel.

Amy Stewart
Amy is a freelance copywriter by day, writer of feminist, speculative fiction by night. She recently completed an MA in Creative Writing at York St John, and is currently studying for a PhD at the University of Sheffield centred around female circus artists. Amy's work can be found in the Aurora Journal, Ellipsis Zine and the upcoming Test Signal anthology from Bloomsbury and DeadInk Books (July 2021). In 2019, she received a Highly Commended Award in the Bridport Prize for her short story, *Wolf Women*. She's most often found ambling around the Yorkshire countryside with her partner Phil and rescue dog, Wolfie.

Daniel Gustafsson
Daniel has published volumes of poetry in both English and Swedish, most recently *Fordings* (Marble Poetry, 2020). New work appears in The Brazen Head, The North American Anglican, and Trinity House Review. Daniel has a PhD in Philosophy from The University of York. He lives in York.
Twitter: @PoetGustafsson

Emily Black
Author of The Life Chronicles: a creative writing column for RAZZ Magazine, Emily's work has appeared in Enigma Journal, The Founder and Exeposé. She assisted in the publication of The Riptide Journal Vol.12. From the South East of England, Emily is currently studying an MA in Creative Writing, in Bloomsbury, London. She has a particular interest in the gritty undercurrent of the everyday, the relationships between people, and how our most unfathomable desires manifest in the pauses before we speak.

Kitty Greenbrown
Kitty is a spoken word poet with a keen interest in telling stories and collaborating with artists and musicians. She's a Say Owt Slam and York Culture Awards winner, and has recently been awarded funding by the Arts Council to deliver a VR Poetry project with Explore York. Other recent projects include interruptive performances for York Art Gallery, a digital poetry trail for York City Council and Rust for the Great Yorkshire Fringe. Her poem *The Incidentals* was recently highly commended in The Poetry Archive's World View 2020 competition by judge Imtiaz Dharker.

Laura Turner
Laura is a poet, playwright and screenwriter passionate about exploring emotion-driven narratives that ask questions about who we are today, often through the lens of the past. Laura has had more than 40 theatre plays produced across China, UK and Europe, and has worked with many screen production companies including the BFI and the BBC. Laura currently has several film and television projects in development and she is a member of BAFTA Crew, Badass.Gal and the European Cultural Parliament's Future Generations initiative, and a Finalist in the Women of the Future 2021 Awards. She runs a poetry Instagram @furypoetry.

Lauren Sharp
Lauren is in her final year studying Creative Writing at Roehampton University. She enjoys finding interesting moments to write about and her work has been published with Fincham Press and online at Bloom Magazine. Her short story, *Burst*, explores the theme of isolation.

Neil James Hudson
Neil is a writer of unrealist fiction who recently graduated with distinction from the York St John Creative Writing MA. He has published around 50 short stories and is currently working on a novel-length story cycle: *One Hundred Pieces of Millia Maslowa*. More information can be found at www.neiljameshudson.net.

Robert Powell
Robert lives in York. As well as short stories, he has produced four poetry collections - *Harvest of Light*, *All*, *Riverain*, and *Aura*, as well as an artist book, two short films, and a pamphlet: *Notes From a Border River*. His work has been widely published in the UK and Canada.
www.rjpowell.org

Rosie Driffill
Rosie is a writer and psychotherapist from North Yorkshire. Her memoir *Suddenly, While Living* – a book that unpicks the challenges of living with an illness that doctors don't understand – was published by Valley Press in January 2021.

Illustrations:

Hekla | Mim Robson
Queen Wasp | Mim Robson
The Fox | Marina Phoont
Burst | Marina Phoont
Seen | Marina Phoont
24 Hours in a Ghost Town | Marina Phoont
Collection | Mim Robson
Galaxies | Marina Phoont
Leaving May | Holly Barratt
Beyond the Storm | Holly Barratt
The Artist | Marina Phoont

Subscribe today, and support new writing.
Includes free postage.

One Year (four issues)
£25

www.theyorkjournal.com